RED SKY

Recollections Of The International Hotel

Emil A. De Guzman

Graphic Design by Amor Aggari
Cover Art by Jack Loo

Printed in the United States of America

First Printing: 2024
Third Printing: 2025
ISBN 978-1-961562-09-7

EAST WIND BOOKS OF BERKELEY

Published by Eastwind Books
2022 University Avenue, Box 46
Berkeley, CA 94704

Email: eastwindbooks@gmail.com

www.AsiaBookCenter.com

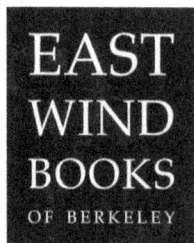

Contents

Dedicated to:

———◆◇◆———

Emilio C. De Guzman Sr.

Teodora A. De Guzman

Maggie De Guzman

Dr. Sarah Maya De Guzman

Emil Kawayan De Guzman III

Photography by Crystal Huie

Long Live the International Hotel.

Those shaping, designing, editing and production
of my book I want to thank:

Magdalena De Guzman

Amor Aggari

Joselyn Ignacio

Harvey Dong and Eastwind Books

Chris Fujimoto

Ira Nowinski, Photographer
(Images Courtesy Associate Librarian and
Director Collections Stanford University Libraries)

Bob Hsiang

Crystal Huie

Nancy Wong

Henry Der

Carol De Guzman

Foreword

Well-financed, private interests never hesitate to shove low-income, racially diverse community members out from their neighborhoods if there is the opportunity to develop the land to increase private wealth. In 1968 the owners of the single-room International Hotel in San Francisco Manilatown on Kearny Street made such a move to evict the tenants, most of whom were Filipino male immigrants who had already endured decades of racial discrimination in California's agricultural fields and other workplaces. Emil De Guzman's **Recollections of the International Hotel** details how key forces, including the tenants, Filipino student activists, and diverse allies from throughout the Bay Area, converged to protest and resist eviction for nearly a decade. Although elderly I-Hotel residents eventually suffered the indignity and trauma of eviction in the middle of the night, they and their supporters remained determined to struggle against corporate interests.

As a student activist, tenant association member and then community leader, De Guzman shares how the coalition of tenants and their supporters strategically pressured public officials to prevent commercial development on the I-Hotel block, and successfully secured public fundings to build replacement housing for displaced tenants and other low-income seniors. No less important, De Guzman emphasizes why the Manilatown Heritage Foundation was created so the memories of Manongs and their struggles against racial discrimination in the broader society are not forgotten. Recollections poignantly captures why a 36-year struggle against corporate interest succeeded: "The I-Hotel was more than a housing movement, it was a revolutionary movement in the belief of human justice."

Henry Der
CAA Oral History Project

Introduction

The International Hotel was a land struggle waged in San Francisco's Kearny Street Manilatown community. The elderly tenants' eviction by a foreign capitalist Four Seas established a property ownership rights triumph to occupy the land formerly occupied by the Filipino community. A parallel analogy can be made when the Pilgrims landed on Plymouth Rock in December 1620. Their foreign occupation in the new world led to displacing Indigenous people on land they had lived on for the millennium. Their land was ultimately stolen by white settlers who proceeded to establish property rights ownership throughout North America.

I wrote this book because no summary of the International Hotel had been written to reflect profoundly recollections of my own involvement. I owed it to the tenants who were in my community to voice their stories of how they lived and led a struggle. I served with them to build an organizational resistance against the incursions that destroyed and upended their lives. Poor and without families, the mainly men and few women embarked on a path to rebel against an unjust system that demonized their dignity as human beings. Rather than live a peaceful and safe life in their late years, they became outcasts subjected to a brutal eviction at their most vulnerable moment ending in a shameful tragedy. I was a beneficiary of their legacy as I learned to embrace their kindness, humility, intelligence, hope and wisdom. I had the privilege of being in an organization with them when we needed each other most to defend our home.

Writing was personal for me. My father Emilio C. De Guzman was a Manong who served in the US Navy for twenty five years. I could imagine the anguish, fears, insecurity, self doubts and hesitations he endured in a powerful American structure with steeped racial divisions and segregation. Proud of his career in the US Navy, he worked hard to earn his promotions achieving the rank of Chief Petty Officer but his only job was as a servant for white naval officers. Like African Americans and Filipino navy seaman, all were assigned the most menial jobs. My Dad's life paralleled the lives of the Manongs. When I understood this, it settled in my mind the trajectory to organize the International Hotel.

Hopefully this book will enlighten the reader of the tangibles, intangibles and intricacies of the international Hotel tenants cherishing their collective role and responsibility. Understanding the essence of a mindset to persevere even as the odds were stacked against us. We praise and memorialize them as heroes, while their adversaries are erased to the dustbin of history.

I came to know that in many ways it was a crime to be Filipino in California .... I feel like a criminal running away from a crime I did not commit. And this crime is that I am a Filipino in America.

Carlos Bulosan

He who does not know how to look back at where he came from will never get to his destination.

Jose Rizal

Chapter 1
Spark that Lit a Prairie Fire

This narrative is a comprehensive summary of the major actors in the eviction of the International Hotel (IH) tenants and destruction of the Manilatown Kearny Street Filipino community. Of the many housing struggles fought in San Francisco history, none were as paramount nor as long as the International Hotel housing struggle to resist a government eviction. The genesis of the IH tenants struggle began in October 1968 and raged for 9 years until it ended with the forced removal and defeat in August 1977. Two years later, the building was demolished leaving an empty hole in the ground. Filipino and Chinese elderly were thrown into the streets with nowhere to go and abandoned by the City's refusal to provide simple aid to relocate them. The horrendous trauma to their personal health and safety, the separation from their compatriots, community and home led to hampering their long lives after the eviction. The violence and persecution for their defiance unmasked the hypocrisy of human rights as an empty and meaningless backdrop against a property class in the capitalist system.

The battle was fought long and hard by the tenants in concert with the displaced poor and working class communities. Nothing can erase the horror of that time but one can learn from the history of housing as a basic human right. It was an attack against the poor and dispossessed they chose to defend.

The I Hotel inspired other housing movement resistances across the country in defending themselves against total annihilation. These were just a few of those

Wahat Tompao, Treasurer IHTA War veteran US Navy retired
Photograph by Chris Fujimoto

struggles: King Dome in Seattle International District, Ota Camp in Honolulu, New York Chinatown, Los Angeles Little Tokyo, Oakland Chinatown, Chinatown Boston, Massachusetts, and Committee Against Nihonmachi Eviction (CANE) in San Francisco Japantown. The International Hotel became a symbol defying the immense power of capitalism's wealth to crush those opposing their rule.

When an old man dies, a library burns to the ground.

African proverb

Educated or not, you don't have rights to disrespect anyone.

Jack Ma

Chapter 2

The History of the International Hotel

The International Hotel struggle began in October 1968 when ground was laid decades earlier. Shortly after 1920, tens of thousands of Filipino young teenage boys and men landed on American shores (some women came, but few). They were crammed onto ship hulls of large commercial vessels then transported to US ports: Seattle, San Francisco and Los Angeles. In California, they proliferated to the Central Valley in towns like Stockton, Delano, and Turlock. They spread to the Central Coast and Coachella Valley. They were met with racial violence, unjust laws of discrimination that violated their rights as immigrants. They were relegated to the social and economic bottom because of their skin color and foreign status.

In the 1920s, San Francisco's Barbary Coast was populated by Europeans, Chinese and Japanese in its northeast section. Single room occupancy tenement hotels housed young Filipinos on Manilatown Kearny Street adjacent to the Barbary Coast. Manilatown became the center of Filipino migration. They lived in and out of the district because their travels working in agriculture to plant and harvest fruits and vegetables required them to migrate around the West Coast performing seasonal farmwork. Work was all year around requiring finding jobs. Travels took them everywhere on the West Coast and Alaska to work in canneries where they canned salmon year after year. Their only job opportunities were when they arrived working in the most backbreaking and hazardous industries at low pay.

Carlos Bulosan gave a description of young Filipinos travels and jobs in his book *America is in the Heart*. His words were his own describing the experiences of his generation living in dangerous times. Riots and jailing even death was the miserable landscape the Manongs faced. But not all was hateful. Joe Talaugen, a Filipino farmworker's son shared what a Japanese farmer told me. Many farmers favorably hired Filipinos as reliable, responsible and efficient. They worked the crops and transported them to market on time. Another farmworker's son Roger Galeano, described picking grapes was not an ordinary, nor easy job. You had to be skilled to pay attention on how table grapes grew. Even in their late age, the elderly bachelor Manongs picked grapes and provided the care of the fruit as if they were their children.

But, housing for Filipino farmworkers was another story. Poorly built housing was unsafe. Joe Talaugen sadly spoke of the death of his father and uncle in 1969 when their shack burned down due to illegal wiring, violating county housing codes. Neglect in camps and ranches was common causing the deaths and injury to farmworkers even families.

This is a great country, but fortunately for you, it is not perfect. There is much to be done to bring about complete equality. Remove hunger. Bring reality closer to theory and democratic principles.

Thurgood Marshall,
Distinguished US
Supreme Court Justice

Service to others is the rent you pay for your room here on earth.

Muhammad Ali,
World Heavy Weight
Boxing Champion

Chapter 3
Post-War Period

1945 gave rise to global transformation of the world order. The United States became the top superpower monopoly capitalist and imperialist system to shape the globe by dominating international trade, global finance controls of emerging new and independent countries. And with western nations reconfigured the global order with peaceful coexistence with the Soviet Union.

Although the Philippines was no longer a colony after 1948, the deployment of US troops and ships on military bases on Subic Bay Naval Base and Clark Air Force Base was evidence of US political and economic influence. The Philippine government loyally complied with US foreign and military policies in the region.

Filipinos in San Francisco found new freedoms in the post-war era. Denied the rights and privileges years before, the doors opened as American laws were reversed with the emergence of the civil rights movement led by Black leadership. Filipinos became naturalized citizens, this opened up property ownership and business startups. Second wave war brides married to Filipino veteran service-men housed families and children who became educated, assimilated into schools in America. This post war born generation received greater opportunities than their parents. One example were the jobs in the public and private sectors as the American economy rapidly grew. Education was a guardrail that gave Filipinos upward mobility.

Yet, not all Filipinos found prosperity in the new age. Those left behind in a fast growing America were the Manongs. Forgotten was their contributions to America as the first wave in an expanding and prosperous America. They suffered from the prewar period of American society, hardship, lost opportunities, segregation and deprivation because of their race. The toll toward their lives manifested into loneliness, poverty, and marginalization even within the Filipino community. There was no advocacy for Manilatowns and Filipino towns to improve the quality of life. The Manongs were usually in the oldest sections of the cities or towns destined for moderation and redevelopment. The vast majority never returned to the Philippines never to see their homeland or families again.

Pity the poor nation whose people are sheep
And shepherds mislead them
Pity the nation whose leaders are liars
Whose sages are silenced
And whose bigots haunt the airwaves
Pity the nation that does not raise its voice
Except to praise conquerers
And acclaim the bully the hero
And aims to rule the world
By force and torture
Pity the nation that knows
No other language as its own
And no other culture than its own
Pity the nation whose breath is money
And sleeps the sleep of the too well fed
Pity the nation pity the people
Who allow their rights to erode
And their freedoms to be washed away
My country tears of thee
Sweet land of liberty!

Lawrence Ferlinghetti

Chapter 4
Pacific Rim

San Francisco became the command center of the Pacific Rim to all Pacific Ocean countries. The label Manhattan of the West was in keeping with its downtown resemblance to New York Wall Street. The city's downtown required more land to make way for high-rise office buildings. America was on the move to rapidly expand its economy by the vast networking of banks, insurance, corporate offices and law firms. By the 1950s, Kearny Street was transformed eliminating the tenement hotels and Filipino businesses. Like the Yerba Buena in the southern section and Fillmore, all was leveled to make way for the city's changes and the losers were the displaced residents of the working class. The city masterplan by the Planning Department and Redevelopment Agencies designed San Francisco's masterplan changes to suit the capitalists plan for a corporate landscape. Kearny Street Manilatown, Japantown, Fillmore, Yerba Buena South of Market were transformed by every conceivable method to disappear either through legal lawful force or criminally illegal methods like torching buildings. Eminent domain, arson and fires to burn tenants or

Skills can be taught. Character you either have or you don't have.

Anthony Bourdain

Victory comes from finding opportunity in problems.

Sun Tzu

An evil man will burn his own nation to the ground to rule over the ashes.

Sun Tzu

even murder was rampant in the city's displacement. By 1969, Kearny Street Manilatown was just one hotel standing on its last block.

Luisa Dela Cruz, Leader IHTA, jewelry box worker, former labor organizer Philippines

Photograph by Ira Nowinski

Claudio Domingo, US Army war veteran, Anecelto Muniz, Tenant.

Photograph by Crystal Huie

Chapter 5
Asian American Era

The 1960s was a significant post war generation period. The Free Speech movement at UC Berkeley, the Viet Nam protest, the sit ins of auto row and hotels in downtown San Francisco. The Civil Rights era gave rise to an awakening consciousness of the injustices and inequality deep seeded in American society. Non violent protesting was a convergence of labor, anti- war, women, students, civil rights and Black power that swept the nation. Minority communities were at the bottom of the social and economic ladder and protesting and marches gave rise to call for freedom to end past injustice and inequities. This massive shift in American politics was an all encompassing wave that exploded everywhere led by the post war generation.

American Asians became aware of the Viet Nam War that the Vietnamese were Asians like themselves. Attacks against Asian Americans began to happen sporadically, especially by veterans who had come back from the war. The news media portrayed the horror of the war in Southeast Asia with bombing, massacres, invasions by American military troops on television.

This sparked a furor by the American people to take to the streets, but deeper was the reflection of the war on Asian American consciousness. The Viet Nam War and the Black Civil Rights movement triggered a politicization of Asian Americans to break out of their lowly status to embrace the anti war and African American freedom movements. The 1960's was the origin of an Asian movement that joined the mainstream of American politics.

Every corner of the country was marked by an Asian American political movement. Asian Americans rose from below the undercurrent to create a national movement of empowerment. A political power identity formed that challenged the injustices, mistreatment, abuse and exploitation in our communities that characterized our collective historic past. Women, workers, children stereotyped as docile and weak were promoted as masters of our own destiny.

Joe Diones, Manager International Hotel
Former International Longshoremen and
Warehousemen Union organizer

Photograph by Ira Nowinski

Once weapons were manufactured to fight wars. Now wars are manufactured to sell weapons.

Arundhati Roy

Our prime purpose is to help others. And if you can't help them, at least don't hurt them.

Dalai Lama

Chapter 6
Student Militancy

For Asian Americans, it was inaugurating the Third World Strikes at San Francisco State and UC Berkeley that many connected their awareness to American injustices. The convergence of nearby Bay Area universities led by students of color victoriously won an amazing, unprecedented demand that broke with white academic tradition in higher education and pedagogy. For the first time, the rights of people of color was established to pursue scholarship in the elite academic echelons severing with the white western constructs of American higher education. The establishment of Ethnic Studies was an admission that racial disparities existed because of the permeating hegemony of white supremacy in all major fields like social sciences, health, law, education. This was paramount to holding back learning leaving behind and dismissive serious studies to raise communities of low social and economic standing from the bottom. The creation of Ethnic Studies was a welcome start to professionalize and dignify scholarship of people of color in a pluralistic and diverse world. Resources and funding for research, scholarly study and training of scholars long

The comfort of the rich depends upon an abundant supply of the poor.

Voltaire

There is only one solution if old age is not to be an absurd parody of our former life, and that is to go on pursing ends that give our existence meaning.

Simone De Beauvoir

UC Berkeley and UCLA students with I Hotel tenants. 1970

Photograph by Anonymous

denied was granted legitimacy to grow and prosper in a higher education environment. Fifty-five years since the founding, Ethnic Studies has been established and is now taught in high schools and middle schools. In California, California law requires students cannot graduate if they do not pass an ethnic studies class.

Chapter 7
Manilatown

The young student generation found moorings once the Asian American identity became an organized force in the International Hotel fight against removal from their home and community. The UC Berkeley Third World Strike infused a revolutionary spark into the struggle. The aging of the elderly Filipinos and Chinese gradually declined in numbers in their community in the late 1960's. Hotels Bell, Clay, Royal, Pine were condemned and demolished as their elderly occupants passed away. The Financial District high-rises replaced the grand past of Manilatown's bars, restaurants, barber shops and small business establishments. Gone were our Manongs standing on the sidewalks chatting and smoking their cigars so frequent the images of the past.

The reality hit me as a college student when my Ninong's (godfather) photography shop closed. Housed under the Palm Hotel on the corner of Kearny and Washington Streets, his building met the same fate of the wrecking ball. The Palm was torn down to make way for a parking lot. Today the San Francisco Community College replaced it on the same exact site. This left the International Hotel as the last hotel standing on the block in 1970.

Colorful organizations, non profits and community organizations inhabited Kearny Street. Lucky M pool hall owned by Margaret Muyco and her husband Uncle Johnny, Silver Wing Restaurant owned by Mamie and Jimmy, Tino's Barber Shop by Tino Regio, Mandalay Bar, Patty Wagon Nightclub, Everybody's Book-

Larry Itliong, Assistant Director United Farmworkers Union
Leader American Workers Organizing Committee

Photograph by Harold Filan

store, Mabuhay Restaurant, Leeway Legal Services, Asian Community Center, Chinese Progressive Association, Mike's Barber Shop, Bella Union movie theater, Jay's corner store, Kearny Street Workshop, Manilatown Multi Service Center, Jeannie and Scottie Bataan Lunch, Star Lunch,. New Cup coffee shop, and Lays Hardware store. Dimasalang Del Trabajos Brotherhood National Headquarters, Nancy and Vicky Cafe and, formerly the famous Hungry I Nightclub was in the basement. The basement later housed a garment factory that closed after the water damage from the fire in 1969.

Chapter 8

The Murders

Joaquin Legaspi, Founder United Filipino Association

Photograph by Danilo T. Begonia

In the early morning hours of March 16, 1969, three tenants Pio Rosete, Marcario Salermo and Robert Kanuff were killed in a mysterious fire that was never solved. Their names are etched in highest esteem for their sacrifice. Their deaths sparked the long battle for the International Hotel housing struggle. Their murders set into motion the human carnage and burgeoning revolutionary mass movement that led to the ultimate eviction. On the night of March 16, an intruder set fire to a room and left the hotel leaving behind a smoldering fire. Smoke filled the hallway forcing tenants to break in. Kicking in the door triggered fresh air causing an explosion killing the three tenants instantly. That night, a battalion of firemen and trucks put out the raging fire. The entire third floor of the northern wing was destroyed and was compounded by heavy rains the next morning. Evacuated and homeless were the second floor tenants. The commercial spaces on the ground floor and basement were emptied and closed for business. A horrible sight and among the damage were the bodies of the three tenants who were dead.

As a result of the heavy damage and huge cost to repair the hotel, next was the City's red tagging of the building for demolition. Whoever was the mastermind behind the fire committed a crime and had one objective to empty the building paving the way for demolition. The City rejected the demolition application. The Board of Permit Appeals rejected the owner's application allowing the resumption of the Hotel operations as long as the building's damaged wing was corrected to meet the building code standards. The owners one victory was the collection of fire insurance. No insurance money went to the victims' property losses. Stopping the demolition was significant allowing the United Filipino Association(UFA) to take possession of the I Hotel.

The tenants were at a disadvantage given their age in the beginning. But the students from the Third World strike victory at the UC Berkeley campus was an infusion of combustible energy and political activism to jumpstart the tenants resistance. An inter-generational bond began to ground the militancy of tenants and students together as one fighting organization. This slowly attracted the public's newsworthy attention that adversely framed the owners as greedy landlords. Furthermore, owners were cowardly as daily pickets outside their downtown offices scared them to run away embarrassed and shamed. Loud demonstrations and non-violent protests were very effective. Two months after the fire, the owners caved in to pressure and negotiated a lease with the United Filipino Association (UFA). The terms were a three year at $40,000 a year payment. The UFA took possession July 1, 1969. Tenants and students entered a new era running a hotel business not for-profit but to maintain the affordability and preservation of a safe and decent housing for the community.

The strategy was simple, resist any encroachment to evict and protect the tenants' home from harm; legally defend and sue the owners in court. One of our heroes was Deputy Director Larry Itliong of the United Farmworkers Organizing Committee. He became involved by referring the Center for Community Change (CCC), the foundation in Washington DC to get behind the tenants struggle. CCC became a partner to negotiate with UFA by guaranteeing the 3 year lease. Larry's helping hand was a key contribution in saving the International Hotel from the wrecking ball.

The warrior is not someone who fights, for no one has the right to take another life. The warrior, for us, is the one who sacrifices himself for the good of others. His or her task is to help care of the elderly, the defenseless, those who cannot provide for themselves, and above all, the children, the future of humanity.

Sitting Bull, Chief of the Lakota Nation

---

1 The UFA was an association representing the elderly Manongs living in Kearny Street Manilatown.

International Hotel-Empty shell, ready for demolition

Photograph by Ira Nowinski

Love, friendship and respect. Do not unite people as much as common hatred for something.

Anton Chekhov

Chapter 9
Outcomes

In reviewing the history, one must take along view the outcomes and consequences of the 57 year span.

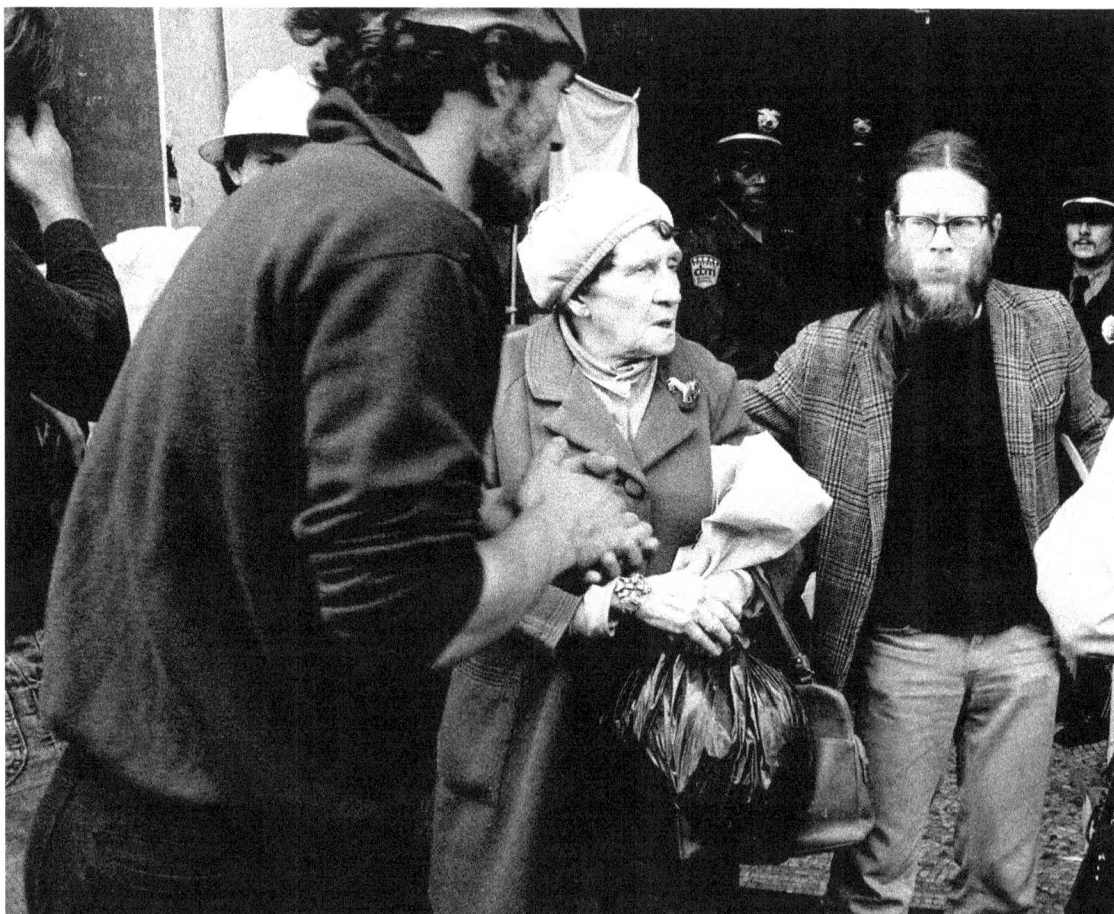

Katheryn Knowles, Tenant with dog Rex

Photograph by Chris Fujimoto

First, it was a protracted battle. After the UFA and the owners signed a contract in 1969, the owners Milton Meyer Inc. expected failure after the three years lease period. They expected the tenants to be delinquent in monthly lease payments. This backfired because the operational costs were manageable. The day-to-day operations and construction was performed by volunteers, students and community friends. There was no outstanding labor costs and no overhead by staffing the maintenance and repairs.

Furthermore, there were ample numbers of people who came to I Hotel to rent affordable housing rooms in the I Hotel which generated a constant revenue stream.

Second, prior to the first eviction notices posted in October 1968, the owners had intentionally disregarded repairs. Years of neglect to the building's safety and integrity with accumulated decrepit furniture, lead paint peeling in the halls and rooms made it quite dangerous for habitation. When the UFA took possession, they became shocked at how blighted it was contributing to the Manongs' ill health. In those early years, the response for cash, fresh paint, furniture, beds and dresser drawers was generous to raise the standards decency and habitability for all the residents. Community Saturdays were gatherings of young supporters, recruited students from nearby and far way college campuses and community to be the workforce to rehab the building. Removal of all the old carpets were thrown out, damaged mattresses/box springs were dumped, chest drawers and broken mirrors were replaced by newer furniture. The miracle transformation brought a sense of dignity and confidence to the tenants and community who acquired control of their destiny, A hotel's ground floor room was an empty storage space, It was discovered and converted into a recreation hall where weekly Sunday brunches brought people together, Even a big wedding of Bill Sorro and Guiliana Milanese was celebrated in the hall. Recreation programs included outings outside San Francisco to beaches, forest and parks where tenants could congregate. All this brought a strong community inside and outside the hotel.

Third, in time the old building had a new look and feel, a spirit of a community connected everyone to one another. The traffic of college and high school students, unions, churches, non profits was welcomed, even foreigners who heard about the International Hotel came to San Francisco to see for themselves. These remarkable changes created a synergy and hope of invincibility to live forever hoping the owners would drop eviction. Flowers and plants decorated the light wells. Dancing and parties during the holidays were celebrated galvanizing the spirit of the tenants to face down the threats against them.

The Center for Community Change, a foundation in Washington DC donated a substantial gift to repair the four floors of the fire damaged northern wing. Golden Spear, a Black construction company, was hired to construct a new roof, perform reconstruction of the second and third floor rooms for occupancy to meet the city's housing codes. The completion added to the hotel business operations revenue stream to meet the monthly lease payment with more rooms and availability of commercial spaces. This maximized the revenue to make improvements and safety measures. Tenants and volunteers worked together daily to run the hotel business operations efficiently and systematically. The owners' plans for a failed business gave them grave doubts of an early eviction.

The one block Kearny Street between Jackson and Washington Streets on which the International Hotel stood had two pool halls, a parking lot, two barber shops, three restaurants, two bars, an art workshop, a theater, corner grocery store, a hardware store and a bookstore. The IH ground floor commercial spaces added to the community appeal to Chinatown. The first floor commercial spaces were immeasurably valuable to expand services to the Chinese and Asian American community. One formidable opposition was the Chinatown establishment who were all anti communists. Their refusal to rent space to the left organizations was a deliberate attempt to block access into Chinatown. The leftist organizations found ample space to rent in the International Hotel in the basement and first floors. These organizations had a wide following because of their outreach programs. Thousands of people crammed to see films produced by the Chinese government on China weekly. Prior to the historic signing of the 1972 Shanghai Communique between the US and Chinese government, thousands of Chinese people who were cut off from their families came to the International Hotel to see the new China. Asian Community Center and Chinese Progressive Association provided a gateway for overseas Chinese to see a modern China after many years of leaving the 1949 Chinese revolution. Once the signing by Chairman Mao Tse Tung and President Richard Nixon, the International Hotel attracted even bigger crowds.

Strength does not come from physical capacity, it comes from an indomitable will.

Mahatma Gandhi
Lawyer, Anti-colonialist

People always said that I didn't give up my seat because I was tired, but That is not true…..No, the only tired I was, was tired of giving in.

Rosa Parks
African-American
civil rights hero

Chapter 10

International Hotel
Tenants Association (IHTA)

The genesis of the national Asian American movement can be traced to the International Hotel fight for community self determination. It served as a catalyst for communities throughout North America to plant themselves in the community life of cities and towns spreading the Asian American identity movement. On the commercial space was Everybody's Bookstore, Kearny Street Workshop, Leeway, Draft Council, Asian Community Center, Chinese Progressive Association, and Manilatown Multi Service Center. There were the business establishments such as Tino's Barbershop, Mabuhay Restaurant, Lays Hardware Store, Mandalay Bar, and the Patty Wagon Night Club.

SFPD in full riot gear bashing human barricade.
Photograph by Bob Hsiang

When the three year lease was over, the tenants' movement became stronger and broad based following the years before. Operating a hotel business community showed their remarkable skills to professionalize their operations. All this while building simultaneously a political movement of self defense. When time came to negotiate another three year lease, the tenants had three assets in their favor: 1) stronger and militant support. 2) business professionalism, 3) zero balance meeting the annual rent of $40,000 to the owners and a bank account in the black. As a result, the owners' disappointment led them to negotiate a month to month lease under the same terms of the annual rent. The only change was the lease would be under a new name: the International Hotel Tenants Association. The owners caved to the pressure as a result of the tenants success.

On October 31, 1973, the owner sold the property to a Chinese-Thai liquor baron, Supasit Mahaguna, who held land title under the name the Four Seas Investment Corporation. The property transfer had the effect of changing ownership from a local, wealthy capitalist to a foreign Asian wealthy capitalist from Thailand. Four Seas was a Hong Kong company owned by the Thai tycoon. The new owner began hiring a high powered law firm to begin the court procedures to clear the land and evict.

Negotiations with Magahuna for lease extensions proved fruitless. The court ultimately mandated San Francisco Sheriff Richard Hongisto to evict the tenants. Refusing to enforce the eviction order, he was jailed for five days April 1977 for violating the judge's order. He eventually fulfilled the court order and evicted tenants out of the I-Hotel the following August. In this nine-year period from 1968 to 1977, massive public support was the key factor for the series of eviction postponements, numerous court stays, and intervention by local politicians.

Furthermore, the IHTA courageousness navigated the battles with City Hall, the court system and the corporate property elite. With the left militant organizations, popular support flanked IHTA with a coalition of local, national and global following. The remarkable maturation of the elderly tenants, many disabled and even deaf, spoke openly and publicly to muster building support. Their leadership was key in widening and escalating the fight to broaden the base of the solidarity movement behind them.

The years of building the IHTA was painstaking. Politically educating the leading tenants helped them gain their own awareness and traction to demand justice. Their convictions persevered striking terror in the hearts of the greedy foreign capitalist out to destroy them. The tenant leaders had all grown proud of their accomplishments and fortunes over the years readying themselves for the fight for their lives. Their patience had worn thin at the owner as they grew unstoppable, closing ranks to engage in battle.

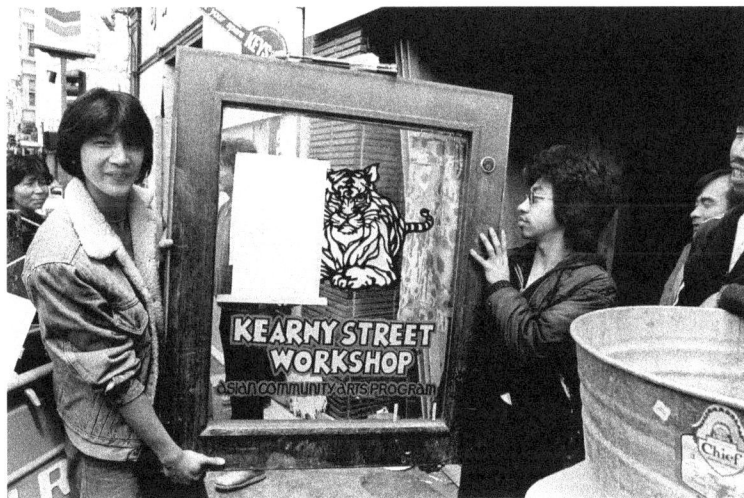

Kearny Street Workshop emptying storefront after eviction

Photograph by Chris Fujimoto

To colonize a people's minds, you have to demonize their culture then their traditions.

Flying Monkey

It is easier to build strong children than to repair broken men.

Frederick Douglass

Chapter 11
Eviction Day August 4,1977

A lie does not become truth, wrong doesn't become right, and evil doesn't become good just because it is accepted by the majority.

Booker T. Washington

An army's fighting capacity is gauged by influencing the final outcome in a battle. That night, thousands formed the human barricade, a partial critical mass of support bravely put themselves in a precarious position against an armed police force. When word came that sheriffs and police were going to attack the I Hotel, the alarm off the phone tree became activated to go and defend the tenants. The numbers began to swell in the hundreds by late afternoon. Tens of thousands were on their way but the police were clever to cordon the outer perimeter of nearby streets to block the people. 300 police and sheriffs were bused in and lined themselves in formations waiting for the signal to march into the crowd. Police on horses began moving in followed by officers on foot behind them. They swung their batons wildly as they charged into the human barricade of defenders standing arm and arm.

The police smashed and clobbered the non violent civil disobedience resistance. Supporters absorbed the blows and jabs of metal batons. Stabs to the bodies and blows to the heads caused major injuries. Amidst violent hammering, the entire scene was a nightmare or war zone lasting into the wee early morning hours. Bod-

Frankie Delos Reyes, Tenants and Russell Robles
Photograph by Chris Fujimoto

ies fell and dropped unprotected from the obstructive energy of pushing and shoving. Bloody and injured people captured the images of the slaughter on streets and sidewalks of Kearny Street. The brutality forced supporters into an orderly retreat to walk south. Meanwhile the police and sheriffs broke into the barricaded hotel and commercial spaces to drag everyone outside. First out were the elderly tenants who were walked down the stairs and out the door with nowhere to go. Saddened and confused with fear in their eyes of where to go and how they were going to survive. Gross overkill and trauma overcast the reaction of tenants and supporters alike of the horror they had just experienced the whole night.

Early morning dawn, they all walked several blocks up to St. Mary's Square on California Street. This was where they rested their tired and broken bodies. Defiant and angry, they promised to return the first chance they could get. They were evicted with only the clothes they wore on their backs and a few possessions. Their rooms were ransacked and destroyed by the raid after they returned. Their lives were shattered and in ruin. That day, the City of San Francisco disgraced itself by destroying a community of elderly whose only purpose was to live out their lives peacefully and in dignity.

Chapter 12
Manhattanization

We need leaders not in love with money but in love with justice. Not in love with publicity but in love with humanity.

Dr. Martin Luther King Jr.

A champion must assemble an army of followers in preparation for a war before it begins. Second, the champion must stand in defense of high moral principles of justice, equity and respect for the rights of all its citizens. Third, a champion must be a shrewd tactician to apply military and information in politics to advance forward and avoid defeat. The combination of the three is an indispensable combination to face an enemy's antiquated movements and power; outmaneuver and prolong timing; apply intelligence skillfully toward exercising tactical movements.

The International Hotel can best be described in this manner. Although the fight went on for a long time, the tenants survived the taunts, legal maneuverings, court decisions, media attacks and acts of sabotage to successfully oppose plans for the eviction. If there was no International Hotel tenants organization there would certainly have had to have one invented. The city's housing crisis was on life support given all the massive inadequate housing that they had neglected to provide. Evictions were commonplace because of eminent domain. The evictions in the Fillmore, and South of Market-Yerba Buena had displaced thousands of San Franciscans.

Afterwards, homes were demolished to make way for the commercialization drive for profits.

The gap widening the crisis was caused by the City's intent to dismantle San Francisco neighborhoods. San Francisco Redevelopment Executive Director Justin Herman cleared 60 square blocks downtown. He is quoted saying, "This land is too valuable for poor people to live there."

Fight for the things that you care about. But do it in a way that will lead others to join you.

Ruth Badar Ginsburg, US Supreme Court Justice

The manhattanization of San Francisco was building more high rises and luxury housing. The property class and downtown aim was for more corporate hotels and corporate buildings to supplement conventions held at the Moscone Convention Center. The City had pushed low income people to leave while city officials were aiming to transform the valuable land into a New York City. They did nothing to address the housing crisis at its most critical stages. Rather than replace the housing stock with new housing, they chose another solution. Launch the police, criminal justice system and planning department to implement their strategy of destruction and displacement. They made life unlivable and used property laws to push poor people to leave their homes. This coupled with the high cost of living and rents made it unaffordable to live in their homes. This has been the trend and continues until today with gentrification in neighborhoods like Chinatown, the Mission, Outer Mission, Western Addition, Excelsior and Mission Bay. San Francisco's inaction contributes to a deepening housing crisis for the poor. This resulted into a massive homelessness that today has exploded.

Chapter 13
Navigating Treacherous Waters

We are born into the world for a purpose and its to make the world a better place.

Minoru Yasui

There are many lessons that can be derived from the International Hotel struggle and tenants fighting back.

First of all, the battle to stop eviction was long and protracted. The City's planning department's grand design to economically develop San Francisco, intentionally left downtown the bottom half of the city's population out of the equation. They were displaced to make way for the modernization without consideration for a constructive and humane solution. Non profit developers were invited to begin to address this as a patch up but not in a genuine grand plan to meet the mounting needs. Instead, luxury housing was priority because you could add to the city's tax base through profiting from owners of expensive condominiums and high priced rentals. This was the City's intent; to expand its revenue with new development. Their logic is you can't make money off the poor. This was the heart of the contradiction.

Second, the tenants were the valued assets at the center of their own struggle. They had to learn how to lead and did so with a steep learning curve that they had to master. Coming from diverse backgrounds as elderly and foreign born immigrants, they were not acquainted with the laws and politics they were embroiled in. They nonetheless had to comprehend the full scope of their dilemma through lawyers and political strategists who had to learn to speak to them at a level to understand. Translations of English into Tagalog and Chinese, primary languages of the tenants, helped them carefully weigh their decisions. The most legalistic court decisions and mundane political abstractions were filtered in this way to move forward. This remarkable attribute could only have happened with deep trust and unity as an unshakable bond working together.

Third, strategy and tactics were very effective while being creative to execute an offensive. There was a solidarity demonstration circling the hotel and across Kearny Street in January 1977. Rumors spread Sheriff Richard Hongisto was going to post evictions on the building. An inmate in the city jail spying for us used the code "eye appointment" for I Hotel to relay to the jail medical staff valuable intelligence picked up from among sheriff deputies conversations. An alarm was passed on through phone tree they were going evict. Instantly, thousands of supporters circled and demonstrated to defend the Hotel. Everybody came from everywhere including the African American and Latino communities to express their solidarity. This sent a signal to City Hall we were ready. It was reinforced by a second mass demonstration two weeks later when thousands came again to thwart another police attempt, A week after, the police went back to the drawing board since every attempt was successfully met by massive resistance. The police response was pitiful. They publicly announced sighting weapons on the roof to call it off. Their announcement was a way not to lose face in face of our defiance. For our side, we knew the police would return and they would make sure they did not fail.

Fourth, International Hotel tenants had a moral imperative. To evict law abiding citizens was sacrilegious and immoral. When you look back from the first eviction notice to the eviction itself, the International Hotel stood on solid ground never to concede or compromise. It was the duty of the City to provide affordable decent housing for its most vulnerable citizens. Facing persecution over their human rights was an affront to their dignity and wellbeing. The legal system was prejudiced to protect an owner's private property which could only happen if the City had fulfilled their responsibility to care for the tenants which they refused to do. Instead the legal system allowed the owners and City to use every device to divide and attack the tenants to turn against each other. This coupled with dividing public support. This failed miserably because the tenants and outside support was solidly keeping the I Hotel whole. The underlying beliefs was housing is a human right. It was this underlying spirit of relations that naturally forged an unyielding movement for justice never to surrender. It was the moral fabric of the tenants character that won over millions who heard of the I Hotel, coupled with the suffering from years of discrimination and exploitation as Asians in America. Filipinos and Chinese lived parallel lives experiencing the racial violence, prejudice and segregation. Most lived alone without family or relatives. The I Hotel was more than a housing movement, it was a revolutionary movement steeped in the belief of human justice.

Give me your tired, your poor, your huddled masses yearning to breathe free, The wretched refuse of your teaming shore. Send these, the homeless, tempest-tossed to me.

Emma Lazarus (1883)

Chinese Tenant on sidewalk among chaos a few days after eviction

Photograph by Chris Fujimoto

Chapter 14
Successful Power Offensive

Anyone can give up; it is the easiest thing in the world to do. But to hold it together when everyone would expect you to fall apart, now that is true strength.

Hannah Arendt

The nine years of tenant possession of the International Hotel was a time honored advantage for the IHTA. Mounting a defense required time to plan a strategy. Time was a big factor to get the understanding, comprehension and immensity to try certain strategies. How best to sidestep the blows of a superior force while preserving and protecting themselves in the midst of a storm. As the battle ensued, the tenants and supporters grew stronger and more confident escalating their tactics and boldly striking at the perception of the adversaries weaknesses to slow them down. We did remarkably well at every turning point, The strategy of power offensive required accumulating strength and momentum to scaffold a sizable mobilization of our forces into action. This harnessed maximizing the fighting capacity to aggressively advance forward. Psychologically this would wear down the superior forces and undermine their planning. The City's bankrupt failure and negligence to build affordable housing was intentionally behind the unjust evictions of vulnerable populations to clear their homes.

The International Hotel tenants stood up for themselves in the midst of a housing crisis. Destroying neighborhoods and displacement of people was unacceptable. Their rally "People First" stood for the greater good and principle to defend themselves and the poor.

Everyone you meet is fighting a battle you know nothing about. Be kind. Always.

Robin Williams

Chinatown supporter marching in Manilatown
Photograph by Chris Fujimoto

Chapter 15
36 Years

Magnanimous dignity, strength, harmony and leadership were hallmarks of the IH tenants struggle nurtured over the years. Public sympathies for their struggle was admirable while the injustices to neglect alternative affordable replacement housing was criminal. The elderly grew stalwart and outspoken in their convictions denouncing the courts and owners while expanding their public adoration.

The entire International Hotel block of community spaces employed the principle of "Serve the People." At the time, "Serve the People" was a slogan for the entire I Hotel block serving the Asian American community. Adopted from the writings of Chairman Mao Tse-tung, "Serve the People" manifested and appealed to the Manilatown Kearny Street Chinatown community. Storefronts on art and culture, a bookstore, a restaurant and bars, jobs and housing built goodwill in the neighborhood. This was the common practice that the International Hotel block lived by.

Massive demonstrations and rallies drew thousands to act in uniting tenant support. Fundraising opportunities enhanced visibility and funded the cost of the struggle. There were no deep pockets, only the massive show of forces dominant in the magnanimous popularity of the tenants housing struggle at a time when the courts denied our appeals while media attacks escalated. In January 1977, the massive demonstration of thousands forced the police to back off eviction because of an alleged gun sightings on the I Hotel roof. This was proven to be a fabricated allegation to save them from an embarrassment of public outrage.

Risks taking was an example of creative thinking by the elderly tenants in the forward motion to fight their struggle. One successful example was the occupation of City Hall in the Spring 1977. One afternoon, twenty elderly Manongs filed quietly into Mayor George Moscone's office room 200 unannounced. Their clandestine act generated controversy in the building. No sooner had they arrived when numerous news media swarmed the outside corridor to cover the surprise stand in. Several hours later, Mayor Moscone met a few tenant representatives in his chamber to talk. They were direct in explicitly demanding him to intervene and stop eviction. After the meeting, tenants marched out with heads high. They told the news media they had achieved their objective to deliver their message to the Mayor. "We Ain't Moving." The tenants maximized their position to shame the Mayor publicly with this surprising act of protest. It was an excellent tactic to leverage our power and enhance popularity and support.

Coalitions play a strategic importance at different turning points in a war. In the nine years and ultimately after 36 years, the entire length of the IH struggle, a succession of shifting alliances proved indispensable in promoting the tenants positioning.

Until the lion learns to write, every story will glorify the hunter.

African proverb

If you are neutral in situations of injustice, you've chosen the side of the oppressor.

Desmond Tutu
South African Anglican Archbishop and Theologian

Chapter 16
Coalitions

Coalitions are formed to shield groups behind a wall, a power wall. The intent is to move the wall as required to willfully know who is on our side and who is on the other side. Many actors in the I Hotel struggle came on stage so shifting IHTA positions was necessary depending on who joined us and who opposed us. As the tenants pressed forward in battle we had to rely on reliable and consistent friends. Alliances were formed but could break in an instant. The tenants had to be shrewd, flexible and independent to remain above the chaos and not fall down. Their comprehension of every court decision and legal opinion, plus the complexity of the politics required objectification and minimizing mistakes. The importance of strategy and tactics is to plan a step ahead by positioning ourselves on the offensive.

George Moscone and the Buy Back Plan

An alliance between the IHTA and Mayor of San Francisco George Moscone was first formed to avert eviction. The Mayor joined the coalition to stop eviction by directing the City's Housing Authority to apply eminent domain to place the I Hotel under city ownership. From the perspective of the tenants, this solved the crisis to replace the ownership of the foreign businessman thus subverting the unlawful detainer lawsuit. Under city management, the longevity of the hotel would be permanently established. But an outcry of betrayal sparked by the leftist supporters trashed it as a "Buy Back Plan." They claimed it would stick the tenants with millions of dollars in loans to take over the ownership which for them was a sellout.

International Hotel, January 1977 demonstration
Photograph by Ira Nowinski

This caused a major uproar and split behind the tenants support for the proposal. To the IHTA, the alliance between the tenants and City was a concrete solution to permanently end eviction. The owner litigated and went to court to fight the City's proposal. The Housing Authority lost their case upon appeal at the lower court and ultimately lost the case upon appeal before the California Supreme Court. This ended the last legal option to save the I Hotel to be converted to public housing. Mayor Moscone abandoned his position to evict. On the eve of the eviction August 4, the Mayor vacationed with his family in Hawaii and washed his hands like Pontius Pilate did to Christ.

You don't give a man a weapon until you teach him how to dance.

Irish proverb

It is better to be hated for what you are than to be loved for what you are not.

Andre Gide
Philosopher

US Senator Dianne Feinstein and the new International Hotel

For seventeen years, the site was an empty eyesore hole in the ground. Something remarkable happened in 1994 when the owners Pan Magna put the property up for sale. The failure to build a high-rise had been stopped when all proposals were rejected by the City's Planning Department. After the eviction in 1979, Mayor Dianne Feinstein formed a Mayor's International Hotel Advisory Committee to focus on the I Hotel property. It was composed of representatives of the Chinatown, the Filipino community and Old St. Mary's Church.

Bill Sorro, former Tenant organizer, ironworker, Manilatown Heritage Foundation Founder, looking at I Hotel empty hole in the ground

Photograph by Ira Nowinski

In 1994, when Feinstein was California's US Senator, she requested the Federal Department's Housing and Urban Development (HUD) to finance a new senior housing on the site. The proposal gained traction when the City of San Francisco, the Catholic Archdiocese of San Francisco, House Congresswoman Nancy Pelosi, Mayor Frank Jordan, and the Filipino and Chinese community joined backing the proposal. This was the coalition that would successfully build the new International Hotel as senior housing. In August 2005, the IH doors were open to a 104 units in a 15 story high-rise structure subsidized by Federal Section 8 monies for affordable housing. The combined total cost of the new building was thirty million dollars financed by HUD and City Mayor's Office of Housing. In addition, the Manilatown Center was created on the first floor of the new International Hotel building run by Manilatown Heritage Foundation. This retains and enshrines the legacy of the International Hotel tenants with photo exhibits and bricks of the old building.

Reverend Cecil Williams Defends the IHTA

In the early morning hours on Kearny Street on June 6, 1977, sheriff deputies raided the front door and stormed throughout the building posting official court eviction documents on the rooms of every tenant's door. It was cause for great alarm as sheriffs flooded the hallways of the I Hotel and quickly exited. It was so early many tenants had not even woken up from sleeping.

The reaction was outrage and anger at the surprise raid. This escalated when Joe Diones, the elderly manager, bragged about even being informed ahead of time. As manager and IHTA president, Joe had been under scrutiny as his management style and leadership as a dictator had been brewing. That morning, he went outside the building for breakfast as was his routine. When he returned, elderly tenants blocked his return at the front door. Not allowed in, he flew into a rage while tenants were enraged at his betrayal. At that moment, Joe was ousted from the International Hotel struggle. He was permitted to remove his property and leave. When news of Joe's ouster was leaked to the press, all hell broke out.

Whoever fights monsters should see to it he does not become a monster.

Friedrich Nietzsche

A slew of TV and news media picked it up. The media took sides and attacked the IHTA by slandering the tenant leadership as communists. They accused young tenants had taken over the IHTA in a coup holding tenants hostage under their control. The press resoundly condemned the IHTA for promoting lies about Joe's removal. The public reaction was shock over Joe's expulsion since he was recognized as the main spokesman. The tenants public image had swung to unfavorable in the turmoil. The press planted grave doubts about the IHTA's ability to lead with its recognized leader ousted. This was a low point in the struggle.

The tenant leadership came up with a brilliant but risky idea. They reached out to a leader in San Francisco, Pastor Rev. Cecil Williams of Glide Memorial Methodist Church. Twenty tenants walked two miles to the Tenderloin and asked to meet him one evening. Reverend Cecil Willliams was a civil rights leader in San Francisco. He was outspoken of his support for the International Hotel. Rev. Williams was close to Joe Diones and expressed alarm at the takeover. In a tense gathering, he heard from tenants about Joe's indiscretions and harmful actions. Under examination and questioning, Cecil listened intently to the tenants complaints. At the end, his perceptions were the elderly tenants did the right thing to take over. It was convincing enough that Cecil sided with the tenants. And it became a decisive turning point. Public acknowledgement of minister's position cleared the air of Joe's expulsion. Nonetheless, the residual effects of the negative publicity had harmed the tenants setting the stage for the eviction to be mounted three months later.

The supreme art of war is to subdue the enemy without fighting.

Sun Tzu, The Art of War

There are more examples of how coalition building became a key factor for the International Hotel support to grow its popularity in the mass movement. The cited examples above were the main turning points highlighting the nine years of struggle.

Manilatown Center and the Filipino Community

The book has been a panoramic synopsis of the importance of the International Hotel and its place in US history. The heroism of the tenants was opposing the injustice and inequality against them by not surrendering to the powerful property class interests and San Francisco City Hall. They fought using nonviolence civil disobedience to build alliances and movements on the principle that affordable housing is a right for all people regardless of age or income. Nobody had the right to destroy their community and they made that clear in their nine years of struggle.

Yet, there is an underlying truth that must be expressed as great as the tenants belief in themselves. Noted must be the credit to the Filipino community for its powerful cover of protection to the tenants struggle. From the very beginning, the Filipino community never abandoned the Filipino and Chinese elderly in quest for justice. There was no countervailing power to crush and annihilate them except the Filipino people and American communities who stood with them. In the hearts and minds of the Filipino people this was a grave injustice that left no choice but to stand together in defiance and fight.

Historically, Filipinos have fought tyranny and colonialism. In 1898, Filipino revolutionaries were defeating the Spanish until America invaded to buy the Philippines as a colony for $20 million. In 1986, the Marcos Dictatorship collapsed because of the Peoples Power movement ending martial law and instituting revival of democracy and a constitutional rights of a free nation.

There can be no separation of Filipinos from these historical events. In our blood is inherent the long tradition for transforming an old world of subservience and inferiority into a new world of freedom and equality. It's this phenomena that drove the Manongs to organize unions and fraternal organizations after the 1920 to combat the racial violence and Black codes against all people of color. The same with calling for the strike in the California Central Valley to unionize all farmworkers for collective bargaining rights and higher wages in 1965. For young Filipino American students, we joined the Third World Liberation Strikes for Ethnic Studies with waves of students of color on university campuses in 1969 to abolish the confinement of higher education.

When early International Hotel veterans and tenants Al Robles, Bill Sorro and I came together in 1994, we decided our mission was to insure the Filipino community was at the table to decide the alternate International Hotel. The other organizations involved were the Archdiocese of San Francisco, Chinatown Community Housing Center, Mayor's Office of Housing, and Mayor's Citizens Advisory Committee of the International Hotel. Our goal was a new affordable housing built with HUD and City money for poor people. This began in 1994 with Federal US Housing and Urban Development providing the funding for the purchase and construction of the new building.

Our outreach attracted many younger Filipinos who became involved. It was an exciting moment because it was reviving the International Hotel spirit of the fight for justice as in the past. By 1996, the Manilatown Heritage Foundation was formed as a non profit (501) C3. In those early years, we advocated for the ground floor of the building to enshrine the tenants' legacy. This was ultimately granted by the new organization formed to own and manage the building International Hotel Senior Housing, Inc. (ISHSI). Manilatown Center is on the first floor of the building. Its purpose is to enshrine the historic legacy as an education center of the International Hotel tenants. If you go to the Center you will see many faces and names in the struggle. At the same time, the Center serves to promote education and cultural programs.

There was a major problem in building the new International Hotel when the building was being completed in 2003. $30 million of Federal and City funds had been allocated to pay only for the 15 story 104 units old housing. How was the money to create the Manilatown Center to be raised? The Manilatown Heritage Foundation was a relatively new grassroots organization whose purpose was advocacy for the new building but with few assets. All our members were volunteers yet composed of eager young people.

We enlisted the advice of Mona Lisa Yuchengco, an influential member of the Filipino community to help us. She suggested a donor and suggested it was not enough for a donor to give a substantial amount to fund the construction. I learned from her that a donor would attract other donors to lead the campaign. At the time, we estimated it would cost a million dollars for the tenant improvements to create the interior design and furnish the Manilatown Center.

Mona Lisa had always been a supporter and so her advocacy on our behalf magnified our reach to the upper echelon of wealthy and resourceful members of our community. She introduced me to Maria Banatao whose husband was Dado Banatao, a Silicon Valley wizard innovator and inventor in Silicon Valley. They offered a fundraiser at their sprawling home at Menlo Atherton. They would invite their Silicon Valley friends and other wealthy friends to a lavish dinner with music. Then they proceeded to make their announcement of a $500,000 match for Manilatown Center. The guests were surprised to generate pledging to match the Banataos gift. It was a major breakthrough to raise all this money in one night. The fundraising was a success raising well over $2 million to create the Manilatown Center.

Some can say that the International Hotel tenants from the start did not have a chance when they stood up to the first evictions in 1968. It was made worse when the three tenants were murdered in the fire by an arsonist whose intent was to demolish the building and evict the people. Who would have thought 37 years later on Kearny Street at the new International Hotel would rise up to house elderly again. All former Mayors of San Francisco who served since the evictions -- Art Agnos, Frank Jordan, Willie Brown and Gavin Newsom were among the invited guests at the opening celebration. How could this miracle happen after so many years. All the credit to keeping the faith alive were the people united will never be defeated by the Filipino community and friends. Power of the People prevailed in the end.

Manilatown musicians jamming at Tino's Barbershop

Photograph by D. P. Gonzales

Chapter 17
Role of the Subjective Forces

The Katipunan ng mag Demokratikong Filipino (KDP) Union of Filipinos was a revolutionary organization that joined the political struggle. We were the cadre members providing direction forward in the battle. In the case of the International Hotel, there were among the leadership skilled KDP organizers whose role was indispensable in the entire nine years of struggle. Some joined the tenants at the time of the fire that killed the three tenants in 1969. Others joined later and some became tenants. The KDP openly worked in the tenants association. As members, they were tenants and volunteers working together. It was their steady and intimate flow of information that became the tangibles to objectify the struggle as it grew and unfolded at every turning point. The KDP unit scaffolded and alerted the dangers and pitfalls in a complex political landscape. Often the tenants association was successful in navigating skirmishes and attacks as the struggle intensified. In face of setbacks, the tenants regained their composure to bounce back to counter attack. It was the KDP's close coordination in the tenant leadership that successfully led the International Hotel struggle over years. The KDP worked in the tenants association IHTA surrounded by a powerful government machinery of law enforcement, the judicial courts, a hostile news media, and the corporate property owners out to crush the tenants to defeat them. They wanted to derail a costly eviction by forcing the tenants to fold. This never happened. The KDP shoulder-to-shoulder with the tenants waged together the battle. And when it happened, they marched together to meet it.

Luck cannot be discounted as a factor in the tenants favor.

Federico Delos Reyes, Banjo player

Photograph by Chris Fujimoto

"And the Moon
said to me -
My darling, you
do not have to
be whole in
order to shine."

- Nichole McElhaney

Emil De Guzman, Bill Sorro and Al Robles, Founders Manilatown Heritage Foundation

Photograph by Bay Area Guardian

FIGHT FOR THE INTERNATIONAL HOTEL

Interview by Chris Chow

Photograph by Nancy Wong

Robert and Emil De Guzman
Ages 6 and 7

Mandares Photography
on Kearny Street

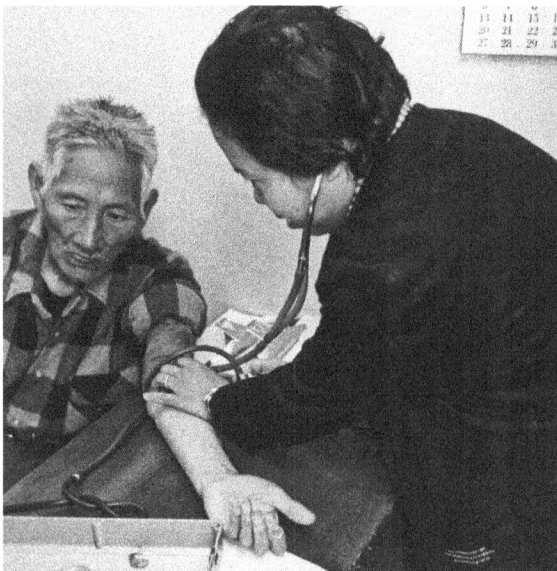

Yee Tung, Tenant Medical examination

Photography by Ira Nowinski

Felix Ayson, Tenant, IHTA Board member

Photograph by Chrystal Huie

MHF Board members Roy Recio, California Attorney General Rob Bonta and Emil De Guzman

Photograph by Emil De Guzman

Joe Bungayan in Lightwell Garden
IHTA Board member

Photograph by Ira Nowinski

Frankie Delos Reyes, Tenant

Photograph by Ira Nowinski

Claudio Domingo, US Army veteran, a martyr of the
I-Hotel struggle

Photograph by Ira Nowinski

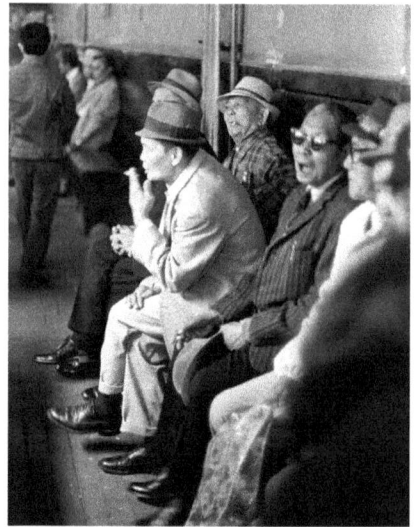

Manongs in Lucky M Poolhall

Photograph by Chris Fujimoto

Anecleto Muniz, Tenant, playing guitar

Photograph by Ira Nowinski

Seaweed, Tenant

Photograph by Chris Fujimoto

International Hotel for Senior Housing

Photograph by Emil De Guzman

Joe Regadio, War Veteran US Army,
IHTA Board member

Photograph by Ira Nowinski

Andres Soria, Tenant; Al Robles, Organizer

Photograph by Chris Fujimoto

Mr. Yip, Tenant

Photograph by Chris Fujimoto

Heroes of the
International Hotel

Police on horses, ramming into human barricade

Photograph by San Francisco Chronicle

United Filipino Association (UFA)

- Joaquin Legaspi, Founder
- Ness Aquino, President 1968-1971
- Rev. Dr. Antonio Ubalde, President 1971-1973

UFA Board of Directors

- Lorraine Wiles
- Pete Marasigan
- Julie McLeod
- Marc Bautista
- Emil De Guzman
- Bruce Occena
- Frank Celada

International Hotel Tenants Association Board of Directors 1972-1977

- Joe Diones
  President 1974-1977
- Emil De Guzman
  President 1977
- Luisa Dela Cruz
- Claudio Domingo
- So Chung
- Etta Moon
- Wahat Tampao
- Felix Ayson
- Joe Bungayan
- Nita Radar
- Lina Blanco
- Harry Young
- Nick Napeek
- Joe Regadio
- Cesario Realin
- Felipe Daguro
- Calvin Roberts
- Pete Yamamoto
- Likeke
- Seaweed
- Frank Delos Reyes
- Raymond Fortunato

Manilatown Heritage Foundation Board of Directors 1996-2010

- Emil De Guzman
- Bill Sorro
- Al Robles
- Dr. Estella Habal
- Rex DeGuia
- Roy Recio
- Sylvia Vivar
- Bruce Occena
- Belvin Louie
- Liz Del Sol
- Jose Toledo
- Evelyn Luluquisen
- Tony Robles
- Carmen Choy
- Desu Sorro
- Caroline Cabading
- Dr. Allyson Tintiangco-Cabales
- Dr. Dawn Mabalan
- Anna Alves
- Rob Bonta
- Frank Celada

KDP Union of Democratic Filipinos Members

- Jeanette Lazam
- Dr. Estella Habal
- Emil De Guzman

International

- Joe Diones
- Nick Napeek
- Luisa and Alfredo Dela Cruz
- Likeke
- Joe Regadio
- Jose Albarillo and family
- Emilio Parades and family
- Fok Ling
- Howard Wong
- Mr. Espiritu
- Claudio Domingo
- Hermie Aquino and family
- Mr. Monte
- Freddie Delos Reyes
- Yee Tung
- Susie Pong
- Anacleto Muniz
- Joe Bungayan
- Cesario Realin
- Peter Yamamoto
- Mr. Agnes
- Felix Ayson
- Raymond Fortunato
- Julio Alabanza
- Don Austin
- Ed Brown
- Lina Burgos
- Frank Cordero
- So Chung
- Etta Moon
- Raimundo Burciaga and Zelma Toro
- Bill Sorro and Giuliana Milanese
- Charles Smith
- Calvin Roberts
- Emil De Guzman
- Felipe Daguro
- Judy Chau
- Yui Chew
- Seaweed

Hotel Tenants

- Antonio De Lucena
- P Esplana
- Eno Forner
- An Gillman
- Johnnie Gonzaga
- Tony Goolsby
- Frank Hill
- Sam Lim
- Mr. Omeat
- Mrs. Katheryn Knowles
- Tex Llamera
- Jeanette Lazam
- Regia Calacal
- Albert Larson
- Ernest Latham
- Joe Lee
- Jew Thick Leung
- Lee Quan
- Rebecca Shaen Leong Yea
- Anacleto Muniz
- Teruko Masumoto
- H Olivera
- Nick Oller
- James Ordonez
- Rafael Paglinawan
- Andrew Roy
- Nita Radar
- Andres Soria
- M. Suen
- Yi So Su
- Romy Santos
- James Walsh
- James Tatum
- Wahat Tampao
- Victor Young Sr
- Victor Young Jr. Ernesto Fonseca
- Antonio De Lucena
- Antonio Serafino

Carlos Bulosan's Poem
I Want the Wide American Earth
(circa 1950)

Before the brave, before the proud builders and workers,
I say I want the wide American earth,
Its beautiful rivers and long valleys and fertile plains,
Its numberless hamlets and expanding towns and towering cities,

Its limitless frontiers, its probing intelligence,
For all the free.

Free men everywhere in my land—
This wide American earth—do not wander homeless,
And are not alone; friendship is our bread, love our air;
And we call each other comrade, each growing with the other,
Each a neighbor to the other, boundless in freedom.

I say I want the wide American earth....
I say to you defenders of freedom, builders of peace,
I say to you democratic brothers, comrades of love:
Their judges lynch us, their police hunt us;
Their armies and navies and airmen terrorize us;
Their thugs and stoolies and murderers kill us;
They take away bread from our children;
They ravage our women;
They deny life to our elders.

But I say we have the truth

On our side, we have the future with us;

We are millions everywhere,

on seas and oceans and lands;

In air;

On water and all over this very earth.

We are millions working together.

We are building, creating, molding life.

We are shaping the shining structures of love.

We are everywhere, we are everywhere.

We are there when they sentence us to prison for telling the truth;

We are there when they conscript us to fight their wars;

We are there when they throw us in concentration camps;

We are there when they come at dawn with their guns.

We are there, we are there,

and we say to them:

"You cannot frighten us with your bombs and deaths;

You cannot drive us away from our land with your hate and disease;

You cannot starve us with your war programs and high prices;

You cannot command us with your nothing,

Because you are nothing but nothing;

You cannot put us all in your padded jails;

You cannot snatch the dawn of life from us!"

And we say to them:

"Remember, remember,

We shall no longer wear rags, eat stale bread, live in darkness;

We shall no longer kneel on our knees to your false gods;

We shall no longer beg you for a share of life.

Remember, remember,

O remember in the deepest midnight of your fear,

We shall emulate the wonder of our women,

The ringing laughter of our children,

The strength and manhood of our men

With a true and honest and powerful love!"

And we say to them:

"We are the creators of a flowering race!"

I say I want the wide American earth.

I say to you too, sharer of my delights and thoughts,

I say this deathless truth,

And more—

      For look, watch, listen:

With a stroke of my hand I open the dawn of a new world,

Lift up the beautiful horizon of a new life;

All for you, comrade and my love.

        See:

The magnificent towers of our future is afire with truth,

And growing with the fuel of the heart of my heart,

and unfolding and unfolding, and flowering and flowering

In the bright new sun of our world;

All for you, comrade and my wife.

        And see:

I cry, I weep with joy,

And my tears are the tears of my people....

Before the brave, before the proud builders and workers,

I say I want the wide American earth
For all the free,
I want the wide American earth for my people,
I want my beautiful land.
I want it with my rippling strength and tenderness
Of love and light and truth
For all the free—

Carlos Bulosan

1913–1956

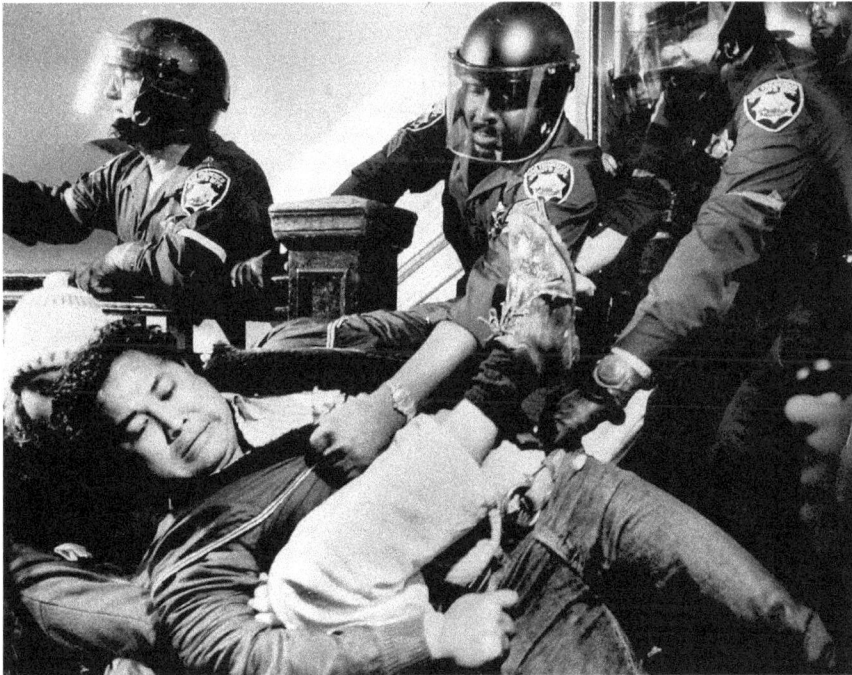

Eviction photo surrounded by Sheriffs
San Francisco, CA ■ August 4, 1977 I-Hotel eviction

1971 Photograph of The International Hotel

Photograph Courtesy of the Manilatown Heritage Foundation Archives

Summer 1985 Seward, Alaska ■ Photographer John Stamets

About the Author

Emil A. De Guzman was born to Filipino migrant parents and grew up in San Francisco. He attended public and private schools. He is a graduate of the University of California Berkeley and Harvard University. Distinguished community and labor organizer over many years. Served in government, non-profit organizations and higher education. Academic credentials include founder and lecturer of Asian American Studies Division UC Berkeley. Faculty member at University of San Francisco, San Francisco State University, California State University Sacramento. President International Hotel Tenants Association 1977, President emeritus Manilatown Heritage Foundation 1996-2010. He owns a small rice farm in the Visayas and home in Manila, Philippines.

"As a student activist and a community leader in San Francisco's International Hotel anti-eviction movement, Emil De Guzman is an important historical figure in Asian American history and the history of social justice movements. Red Sky preserves his recollections of this seminal struggle for housing and human dignity. It should grace the shelves of all institutional and personal libraries that value human rights."

–**Catherine Ceniza Choy**, *author of Asian American Histories of the United States*

"Emil A. DeGuzman's Red Sky: Recollections of the International Hotel is a powerful account of the battle for the International Hotel, the soul of the Filipino community in San Francisco's Manilatownold by the author, who was on the ground as a fierce community advocate and defender. Presented in short, highly readable chapters, the book is appropriate for advanced middle school readers and above. Even well-read adults will find the many details about the struggle remarkable at times gravely grievous, but ultimately, extraordinarily inspiring. The book fills a troubling void in the history of the Filipino community, not only in San Francisco, but across the country. DeGuzman takes the reader from the early days of Filipino migration in the early 20th century, through the valor of Filipino veterans during World War II, to the "Asian American Era" of the 1960s, when Asian American students found their voice to protest injustice. These students took up the cause of the International Hotel Tenants Association, who were fighting corporate interests, City Hall, and eventually, police officers in full riot gear to protect not only community housing, but the very community itself.

DeGuzman describes a "David vs. Goliath" struggle fueled by mass demonstrations and rallies that united tenants, allies from neighboring Chinatown and the Black community, students from San Francisco State University and UC Berkeley, housing advocates, and human rights defenders. While, in the short term, the forces of Goliath appeared to win the battle, DeGuzman writes about how the community managed to reclaim some of its losses and ultimately triumphed in the long war. This book is a must-read for students of Asian American history. DeGuzman has authored a classic that belongs in every library on the challenges immigrant communities face when establishing themselves in this country. In an age where the country is moving rapidly toward a new and sharp xenophobia, De-Guzman reminds us of what ethnic communities have weathered, overcome, and, in the end, how they prevail."

–**Emily Murase,** *Ph. D Stanford University*
Former Executive Director Commission Status of Women City and County of San Francisco

RED SKY

www.ingramcontent.com/pod-product-compliance
Lightning Source LLC
Chambersburg PA
CBHW042347030426
42335CB00031B/3487